Marcus T. Livy

I0116205

STORIES FROM THE BORDER

AND A SOLUTION TO

ILLEGAL IMMIGRATION

Marcus T. Livy

1

The final approval for this literary material is granted by the author.

First printing

This is a true story. All characters appearing in this work are real people. Some dates, places, and names, with the exception of one individual, have been changed to protect their identities.

ISBN: 978-1-951780-00-5 (trade paperback)

Printed in the United States of America

Marcus T. Livy

ONE

Out of all the issues we face in the United States, there are few as divisive as **illegal immigration**. This topic has *intimidated* politicians, created *racial rifts* among our communities, and has left us just as *divided* as we were during the Civil War. And that divide is growing.

Within the last several years, I have heard various opinions, thoughts, and half-measured solutions to illegal immigration. The topic has been taken by the media and manipulated, pulling half-truths to the forefront of the debate. To add even more confusion, the issue has been turned into a political football that is utilized more to score points against a pundit than in making any real progress. Personal stories of violence, injustice, and abuse from both sides of the argument are brought to the forefront, making the opponents on either side seem heartless and cruel.

Well, I want to be one voice among the few to make a single but bold claim:

There is a simple solution to illegal immigration.

The solution I propose does not only protect the interests of the United States and Mexico, but also the interests of the illegal immigrant and the average American citizen. But before I get into that discussion, I want to qualify my assertions. I am not a scholar. I am not a politician. I am not a businessman that makes money off the labors of illegal immigrants; I am not a member of the Sinaloa Cartel that beats, rapes, and murders their own people as they seek a better life.

But I do have a unique perspective and I believe that has made all the difference. I have literally lived on both sides of the map and on the issue of immigration. And it is, I believe, that experience that qualifies me to speak concerning this matter.

TWO

CULIACAN, MEXICO

In December 2003, I decided with several of my friends to move to Mexico. I had volunteered to help as part of a program with my church. Our task would be to help individuals who were struggling with emotional, financial, or physical issues. I thought it was an excellent opportunity for me to help others, learn about another culture, and try to master the Spanish language.

After months of preparation, I took a flight to Culiacan, Mexico—a place I did not know existed until I arrived. This place, I would later discover, would turn out to be an essential location to the Sinaloa Cartel.

I was not prepared for what awaited me. When I walked off the airplane, it was June, one of the hottest months of the year. I was hit with one-hundred-degree heat plus one hundred percent humidity. My body began to perspire in a way I did not even think was possible. Every pore worked overtime as I became a living river. I was later told that the elevation of Culiacan was lower than sea level, and so any coastal breeze drifted far above the city. I have no idea if that is true, but it seemed to make sense to me at the time.

I was greeted by some church counterparts who quickly conveyed to me that my Spanish was unintelligible. I was not told this directly, but every time I said something in Spanish, no one seemed to react. Apparently, my year of Spanish in college did not mean much. I was taken to a two-room apartment with no air conditioning, no dishwasher, no washing machine, no dryer, no water heater, no cupboards, dressers, or couches. It appeared as if the church had rented an apartment that had been recently burglarized. We did have electricity along with a small refrigerator without a freezer, and a set of fans, which I dragged around the house everywhere I went like a faithful Bassett hound.

That night, as soon as I could, I went to the bathroom to take a shower so I could briefly escape the heat. What I found was that the water was frigid—so cold in fact that it was not so much a refreshing shower as it was an experiment in hyperthermia. The only way to heat the water was a small device that hung from the showerhead that would shoot an electrical current through the water. The water then would become scalding. So, the time in the shower was a delicate ballet where I had to switch the electrical device on and off, trying to warm up the water but not so much where it gave me first degree burns.

As I moved the switch back and forth during my first shower, and as shampoo slipped into my eye, I lost my concentration just long enough for my hand to drift into the device. I found myself caught in the electrical current. I would have died with the same amount of clothes and dignity as when I was born had gravity not pulled me free of the device. Moments later, I found myself naked, cold, and on the floor.

I quickly learned several valuable lessons. On my first day of walking through Culiacan, I met a topless woman who answered her door while breastfeeding. I turned a shade of red that day that I do not think I have ever repeated. Lesson learned: different cultures have different perspectives with regards to breastfeeding. Within the first week, I found a live scorpion in my bowl of cereal. Lesson learned: don't leave your food out. Within the first month, I had destroyed all of my pairs of pants as I tried to wash them by hand on a concrete washboard. Lesson learned: use the legs of your pants to scrub the pants instead of using the washboard to scrub the pants directly. Within the first few months, I drank a little water from the tap as I was brushing my teeth and fell deathly ill. Lesson learned: the smallest amount of water consumed from the tap will make you sick for a week.

Of all these adjustments, there was one that surprised me more than the rest. The people of Culiacan were some of the kindest, hardest working individuals I have ever met. Almost every person I ran into, whether they were interested in what I had to say or not, would offer water, food, and conversation. My entire life in the United States, I thought a neighbor was just someone that happened to buy a house next to you. In Culiacan, however, my neighbors were almost family. In my short time in Mexico, I received more invitations to parties and events than I ever did as an undergraduate in college. Despite the poverty, there was always food, laughter, dancing, and friends.

The people were kind, but they were not rich. They made little but shared a lot. Everywhere I went was either on foot or by taking the bus. The buses were extremely inexpensive, being only one peso per ride—the equivalent of .10 cents at the time. Very few families had personal vehicles, and most of them were old beaters that would have been sold long ago for scrap if they were in the United States.

When I was there, the most popular toy in Culiacan was a tropa, which is a sort of top that the kids would use to battle each other. Kids played where they found room, mostly in the middle of dirt roads. The only paved streets were in the city proper. The vast majority of the streets that went between residences were formed by thousands of footfalls over a period of decades. Consequently, rains and floods devastated the roads and driveways. The repair of these roads fell upon those citizens whose homes were no longer accessible. If there was an elderly lady or man that did not have the physical strength to repair the road, they depended entirely on the mercy of others to help them out. And the neighbors always rose to the challenge.

There were no parks, shared grounds where families could gather for picnics, or water parks. There were no forested groves, duck ponds, or planned recreation areas. There were a few dead and dying soccer fields spread throughout the city, but they were overused and crowded. Despite oppressive poverty, the Mexican people tried everything to better themselves. Almost every street had at least one house that had turned their front living room into a small store or "Tienda." In some cases, this was the only source of income for a family. These Tiendas had a tiny profit margin that barely made the enterprise worthwhile. Other individuals would ride around on the back of trucks peddling propane. They would drive up and down residential streets, hitting the propane tanks with a chain to call attention to their goods. Another company drove up and down the streets playing a jingle as they sold purified water.

I remember one day, when I spoke to a family out on the porch in the blazing sun, I met an individual named Juan Medina. Family members told me that Juan was 120 years old. He was blind, deaf, and could barely move. He was in pain when he breathed, when he stood, when he walked, when he ate, when he sat, when he used the restroom.

Within a week, Juan Medina died slowly and painfully as his last moments were spent with the anxiety that accompanies death. The only thing to ease his passing was being surrounded by friends and family.

While I walked the streets of Culiacan, I saw all sorts of mentally ill individuals. With no social safety net, and if family members were not willing to take care of them, these individuals were turned out to the streets, left to die. Sometimes they did simply that, or other times they became predators who preyed on the public.

I enjoyed my time immensely, and I was received with warm hospitality in almost every home I visited. After seven months, I returned to the United States. My Spanish was better, as well as my understanding of the Mexican culture and people. It was then that I came to the conclusion that many of the individuals in Mexico were hard-working, decent individuals who would benefit any community that they belonged to if they were only given a chance.

THREE

YAKIMA, WASHINGTON

I was so impacted by my experience in Mexico, I decided to volunteer for another Spanish speaking church program, this one in Yakima, Washington. I volunteered to help predominantly Spanish speakers who were living in the United States.

When I first arrived in Yakima, I shared a four-room house with several roommates. We had all the amenities I lacked in Mexico, and I was grateful for them. I went about helping people the same way in Washington as I did in Mexico. My Spanish was much better and I could hold lengthy conversations on a myriad of topics. I enjoyed my time there, but it was different. The people I was now working with were almost all illegally present in the United States. Most of them were still friendly but not nearly as open as they were in Mexico. Despite almost none of them speaking English, many were gainfully employed, owned vehicles, and lived in homes that they rented.

After several years of saving, many of these illegal immigrants made arrangements for their families to cross the border and enter the United States. When the families would arrive, they would bring with them horrendous stories of their struggles to cross the border. I heard stories of families running through the desert for days on end with little to no water. Almost everyone I spoke to had been robbed at least once during the process, either by other immigrants who were waiting to cross the border, Mexican cartel members looking to make a little extra money, or by Mexican "rip crews" that operated in the United States. A rip crew is a group of armed individuals that had once been part of a Cartel organization but had been cut out to increase profits at one point or another. They would then use their intimate knowledge of the area and smuggling routes to ambush "drug mules" as they carried loads of marijuana into the United States. A drug mule is an individual that carries illicit narcotics, usually packaged in 50 to 60-

pound bundles, across the border. When a rip crew encounters drug mules, it typically ends up poorly for the mules. If the drug mules resist, they are murdered; if they let their drugs go without a fight, they must answer to members of the associated cartel back in Mexico. Depending on how many loads an individual had lost in the past, they could easily end up dead. Sometimes, however, when a Rip Crew did not run into any drug mules, they would end up targeting and robbing a group of illegal immigrants crossing the border instead.

During the illegal immigration process, rape was as common and accepted as every other abuse. Mexican cartel members would prey on women who traveled alone. These women were often separated from other immigrants, kidnapped, and forced to fulfill every sexual act that was ever contemplated by the human mind. Sometimes, rape became part of the price for being smuggled into the United States; or at any point in the process, a woman could be raped arbitrarily. Even if a woman traveled with her husband, there was little a spouse could do to protect his wife. If he stood up for his wife, he would die. Life along the border was cheap and there was little that Mexican law enforcement officials could do to stem the violence. Many of these rapes were done for sport, such as those that occurred around the infamous "rape trees." If a footguide, the individual who guided immigrants into the United States, raped a female under specific trees spread across the border, they would take the women's bra or panties and throw them up into the branches as a sign of their conquest.

I learned that the price to hire a "coyote"—the nickname for a smuggler or footguide—was usually $2,500 to $4,500. When someone was smuggled into the United States, they were typically held hostage until their debt was paid. Any delay in payment to the cartels often ended poorly for the immigrants who were held captive as slaves, especially if they were female.

Because of their limited financial resources, illegal immigrants in the United States often lived together in small communities in the more impoverished neighborhoods of the city. They were from a myriad of countries: Honduras, El Salvador, Guatemala, Dominican Republic, Cuba, and many more. They would often sleep several people to a room, in conditions that you would expect to see in a third world country.

They took difficult and physically demanding jobs that typically paid 10 dollars an hour, such as roofing, painting, landscaping, cleaning, and various jobs in construction. Some saved money so they could return to their home country, but others wanted to stay in the United States so their children could have better educational opportunities. By and large, most of the illegal immigrants just wanted a fair wage so they could better provide for their children. As more illegal immigrants congregated together, it became more dangerous, especially since illegal immigrants rarely called the police in an emergency. As a result, these enclaves of illegal immigrants quickly became ripe with criminal gangs.

While in Washington, I met Jose and Maria Sandoval and their two children. The young family had illegally moved into the United States four years previously. Despite not speaking English, they had done well, purchasing two vehicles, a house full of second-hand furniture, and a decent-sized home. The father worked endlessly, jumping from construction project to project as he tried to earn enough money for his family. I have never seen another individual work so hard, dutifully rising in the morning and working long hours into the night. With sweat equity, he hoped to purchase a better future for his family.

One day, I stopped by their house to invite them and their kids to a Pinewood Derby sponsored by the church. A Pinewood Derby is an activity where children build small wood cars and then race them. During the conversation, predictably, the kids became animated as they began to make plans for their Pinewood Derby car. The father, however, stared off into the distance, his body more tense then it had been in months.

Eventually, the kids left the room and I was able to speak to the father directly. He did not want to share the news he eventually did. For the last three months, he had been working on a construction project and had not been paid. Every week he went to the employer, the news was the same, "You'll get paid next week." Jose had been judicious with his money and set enough aside in case of emergencies, but now his funds had run out. What food they had in their refrigerator was all the food they possessed. He worried about paying the rent, keeping gasoline in his vehicles just so he could drive to work, and acquiring food for his family. In desperation, he took another construction job in the evening. He was now working sixteen hours a day for six days a week. This second job was also slow in paying their employees. I found out that this was not only a constant problem illegal immigrants faced, it is the norm. As bills for construction projects get paid, illegal immigrant workers were last on a long list.

I suggested to Jose that he report the incident to the police, as this was nothing short of theft. Jose looked at me with an unforgettable smirk on his face that seemed to say, "How can you be so naïve?" Jose explained that he could not go to the police, because they could easily report to Immigration and Customs Enforcement (ICE) that he was illegally present. Even if the police did ignore Jose's immigration status, his employer could make a direct report to ICE with wild accusations about Jose's conduct, and the government agency would be compelled to investigate.

It was disheartening to hear about this family—a family I genuinely cared for—going through a problem that I could not relate to. If someone was withholding wages from me, I'd report my employer to the US Dept of Labor and possibly file a lawsuit. If someone's actions were making it so I could not put food in the mouths of my kids, I'd make so much noise every news and media outlet would hear about it. Jose, on the other hand, had no recourse but to wait and hope his employer would honor their agreement.

Two weeks later, the employer finally did pay, but only after the illegal immigrants banded together and refused to work. It was a bold move, but the employer eventually gave in. When Jose received his check, it was only half of what it should have been, but he accepted it gratefully and without complaint. After the situation resolved itself, I spoke more to Jose about the withheld wages. He stated that this situation was common among almost all illegal immigrants who worked in construction. Even though Jose was already working under a false name and stolen social security number, he stated that he would not want to challenge his employer because it was unlikely his forged credentials would hold up to intense scrutiny. Jose compensated for the occasional lost wages by working two jobs.

I came to the conclusion that illegal immigrants are easy to exploit because they always have the threat of deportation hanging over their heads. And even though many of them get paid "under the table" and taxes are not taken out, it can be very challenging to make ends meet.

13

FOUR

ARTESIA, NEW MEXICO

I graduated from college in 2009, when the economy was in a tailspin. I found that there was fierce competition for even the most basic entry-level positions. I applied for hundreds of positions in my chosen career—law enforcement. I was lucky enough to get a callback, let alone an interview. After months of searching, I applied for a position with the Border Patrol (BP) as a Border Patrol Agent (BPA). Given my experience with Spanish, and my desire to be in law enforcement, BP seemed like a good fit for me. During the next two years, I underwent interviews, written and physical tests, as well as a polygraph. In order to qualify, I had to get Lasik surgery for my eyes. The effort paid off, and in September 2010, I began my employment with the Border Patrol.

My official Entry-on-Duty (EOD) date was September 27, 2010. Trainees, as we were officially called, spent the first day filling out employment paperwork. As we filled out various forms, several of the seasoned Border Patrol Agents (BPAs) acquainted us with the risks and deaths of Border Patrol agents that had happened while in the line of duty. I remember one Border Patrol Agent telling us the story of how a cinderblock was thrown over the border fence as he was performing line watch duties. The cinderblock hit the BP Agent in the face, removing his skin as if it were a mask and knocked him unconscious. He had been rushed to the hospital and his face was stitched back together, as evidenced by the faint scars around his cheeks. We heard story after story of the violent encounters Border Patrol Agents had faced while guarding the border.

The next day, I was up before the sun, boarding a bus that would take us to the Federal Law Enforcement Training Center (FLETC) located in Artesia, New Mexico. By that point, the instructors defaulted their demeanor and tone to that of being drill instructors. In the darkness of the early morning, we boarded the bus without talking and quickly found our seats as instructed.

We were given a final lecture by a BP Agent before being sent off to Artesia, New Mexico. Conversation between the trainees started slowly as we were unsure if talking was permitted. I was sitting next to one of the largest individuals I had ever met. He was built like a lineman but, as I found out later, was as quick as a running back.

"What's your name?" I asked.

"Javier Bustamantes," He answered. "You?"

"Marcus Livy."

As we exchanged our personal histories, he wanted to know what sort of business a "white boy" had down in Culiacan, Mexico.

"I was helping out with a church program," I replied.

He then related to me that he was born and raised in Laredo, Texas, where his first language was Spanish. Thanks to television and elementary school, he quickly learned English. His grandparents had entered the country illegally, but his parents were born in the United States.

The bus ride took several hours, but as we finally approached FLETC, a natural silence fell over the Trainees. I felt my heart pounding into my ribs, my vision sharpening as adrenaline passed through my veins. I had no idea what to expect, and the anticipation of not knowing what was going to happen was killing me. I remember driving through the gates, almost as if going to prison, the guard waving us on with apparent apathy. My fears became realized as a large Border Patrol drill instructor stepped onto the bus. He did not ask for silence, but it was readily given.

"Look at this pile of shit," the Agent announced. "What do they expect me to do with this mess! I haven't seen such a sorry bunch of children since they allowed the local elementary to take a tour of FLETC."

An awkward silence ensued.

Finally, the Agent broke the silence, "What are you still doing on my bus! Get off my bus!"

These words created a sudden sense of urgency that quickly became chaos. We shoved and pushed against each other, fighting our way to the exit as if the bus was on fire. Everything we were instructed to do, we did in earnest, but everything we did, we did wrong. Once off the bus, a dozen Drill Instructors swooped in, as predators before their prey. I grabbed my bag, threw it over my shoulder, and crossed a small patch of grass to line up with those that were in front of me.

"Did you just step on my grass!" shouted one of the instructors. "Me and Moses planted every seed of grass here, and then you come and step on my grass!"

I stopped in my tracks, falling into an unpracticed attention. "Sorry, sir."

"I didn't tell you to stop!" the Instructor replied. "Line up!"

I believe a thesaurus would be impressed with the variety of detailed insults thrown at us as we hurried along. We grabbed our bags, moved to another spot in the parking lot, where we were yelled at for moving too slowly, and were told to return to the spot where we were originally. This took place for some time. We were like school children before a pack of angry Marine Corps Drill Sergeants. One unfortunate trainee packed enough stuff for a family of five. He wrestled with several bags as he tried to move with some sort of speed that would appease the angry gods. At one point, five instructors surrounded him, yelling so loudly the entire campus must have been able to hear them.

That day, while still in our personal clothing, they made us sweat until it dripped down onto the hot pavement in puddles. Pushups, sit-ups, and of course, burpees...the bane of a sane person's existence. In the next few weeks, we were pushed to our limits with constant conditioning of both mind and body. I enjoyed the challenge, the discipline, and the comradery. Any extra weight I had on my body quickly slipped away as it was replaced with lean muscle.

They introduced us to the C-course, and I felt enthralled by the challenge. The C-course is an obstacle course that includes running, wall climbing, balancing, jumping, and crawling. I wanted to be the best in my class at it, but I soon learned my aspirations surpassed my athletic ability. I placed fourth.

As challenging as the physical regiment was, the academic aspect was just as engaging. We learned immigration and nationality law, from the current to the obscure. I quickly learned that our immigration system was a mess. I was amazed at how political and social pressures had evolved our immigration laws until they had become inconsequential and impotent. Immigration had not only been a matter entertained by Congress but one that had been purposely convoluted for various political reasons. Ironically, the majority of my time at the academy was spent in learning Nationality and Immigration law, but it was something I *never* used while in the field as a Border Patrol Agent. Only in the last few weeks of the academy did we do anything that actually resembled what we would be doing on the job. In that week and a half, we arrested "role players" who were pretending to be illegally present in the United States.

One morning in December, while we waited for class to begin, a somber Border Patrol Agent stepped in our classroom.

"A Border Patrol Agent I knew well was just killed by gunfire in the area surrounding Rio Rico," The Agent declared. "This is as real as it gets. Do you still want to be Border Patrol Agents?"

Our class responded with a resounding, "Yes, sir!"

"Are you sure?!?" the BP Agent asked.

"Yes, sir!" Again, the class responded.

"The Agent that died was Brian Terry, make sure you don't forget that name."

"Yes, sir!" we roared one final time.

I remembered repeating the name several times, knowing that Brian Terry had been killed in an area that I would soon be working in. During my time at the academy, we had each been given a card that contained information of a Border Patrol Agent that had been killed. I was surprised to find out that over a hundred individuals had been killed in the line-of-duty since the Border Patrol was first formed.

We were also trained in the use of pressure points, arrest techniques, high-speed vehicle driving, court procedures, interviewing, human tracking or sign cutting, and fighting against multiple assailants. I felt proud on my graduation day, ready to serve next to my brothers and sisters in the Border Patrol. Since I had passed the initial Spanish test, I did not have to stay behind for the Spanish portion of the academy.

In January 2011, I arrived at my duty station in Nogales, Arizona. The first task was to learn the AOR or Area of Responsibility. Our area included a vast swath of land that spread in all directions from Nogales—far more land than could effectively be covered by the 800 Border Patrol Agents stationed in Nogales.

We were assigned On-the-Job Training Officers (OJTs) that were responsible for teaching us the area, how to find and arrest illegal aliens, and how to properly process those that were arrested.

My first arrest happened within the first week of the job. I ran into two men from India who were almost as lost as I was in the strange terrain. It was awkward at first, as they did not speak English well, and I did not know a word of Punjabi. I established that they were present in the country illegally and then placed them under arrest. They were almost as excited to be arrested as I was to arrest them. I later found out that many times, illegal immigrants from China or India often do not care if they are arrested at the border because they apply for and typically receive asylum.

During my career, I processed dozens, if not hundreds, of Chinese and Indian nationals who had been arrested as they attempted to enter into the United States illegally. Processing is the BP term for filling out and completing an individual's "A File" or Immigration file.

I remember one Chinese female in particular who requested asylum for religious persecution. At the time, I was working in the detention area and was responsible for processing the individuals under arrest. Through a program called language-line, an interpreter over the phone translated the conversation. In order to establish the type of persecution she was receiving, I asked her some basic questions with regards to her religion.

"What religion are you part of?"

"Christian," replied the translator.

"What sort of persecution did you receive while in your country?"

"I was passing out pamphlets about Christianity when officials from my government found out and attacked me. They hurt me and told me that if I ever did this again, they would kill me."

The experience she recounted certainly appeared like religious persecution, but in my short time with the Border Patrol, I had already heard the same exact story at least a dozen times by other Chinese Nationals. For some reason, whoever was coaching the immigrants, utilized the exact same story with little to no variation. So, I decided to ask her a question her "coyote" had not planned for.

"Who is Jesus Christ?" I asked.

The illegal immigrant looked confused. With wide eyes, she spoke quickly to the translator on the phone. The translator then relayed the sentiments to me. "This is a new religion for me. I don't know too much about it."

So, this Chinese national, was willing to face religious persecution—even if it meant her death—for a religion that she had no knowledge about. In all honesty, I don't believe I ever processed a single Chinese national who legitimately came to the United States to escape religious persecution.

When an illegal alien is arrested by the Border Patrol, after their citizenship is established, they are transported to an area at the Border Patrol station for processing. During this time, an illegal immigrant is fingerprinted, their eyes are scanned, and their identification and criminal history is established.

The criminal history, however, only shows arrest that occurred in the United States. The National Crime Information Center (NCIC) does not communicate with other countries. So, unless an illegal immigrant had already committed a crime in the United States, a Border Patrol Agent or immigration judge would have no idea what crimes an immigrant had previously committed.

During my time in the Border Patrol, I personally processed hundreds of individuals who had criminal records that ranged from aggravated assault to pedophilia to rape. But since only a small portion of these immigrants committed these heinous crimes in the United States, there were many hundreds more who could have potentially committed these crimes in their native country and a Border Patrol Agent would have no way of knowing.

During another night, an announcement was put out by 865 (865 is the call sign for the radio operators at the Nogales Border Patrol Station). 865 reported that they had just received a distressing call by an illegal immigrant stuck in an 18-wheeler truck. I was assigned King Louis, an area that was frequented by multiple 18-wheelers a day. I called 865 on my cellphone to obtain more details. It was relayed to me that the immigrant had stated he was one of 36 individuals who were being transported into the United States. The illegal immigrant stated that something happened, however, and their driver arbitrarily parked the vehicle and ran off, leaving them trapped inside. He thought that perhaps this was part of the routine, but after hours had passed, and the rising heat of the desert day made the inside of the 18-wheeler unbearable, he began to think something had gone wrong. As quickly as I could, I began to check each 18-wheeler I could find.

They attempted to triangulate the phone call using phone location data, but it showed a reliability rate of 2000 meters. After a while, the immigrant stopped calling, most likely his battery had died. But before he stopped, he relayed that he was not sure if he was still in Mexico or the United States. After several dozen Border Patrol Agents diligently searched, no one was able to find the 18-wheeler. It was likely that the Coyote had staged the truck near the border, but for some reason, he hesitated to drive the vehicle through the Mariposa Port-of-Entry (POE). Given the illegal immigrant's desperation, and the fact that many of them were already out of water when the trapped illegal immigrant first called, it is likely that many, if not all, died of heat exposure. If those 36 immigrants did die due to heat exhaustion, there was nothing anyone in Mexico could or would do about it.

In Mexico, illegal immigrants die all the time. Not only are Mexican law enforcement officers poorly funded and trained, their system is plagued with corruption. If those 36 individuals died in that 18-wheeler, they were likely taken out to the desert and left to rot. No one would come looking for them; no one would care. The country is so corrupt that even if a Mexican law enforcement official made a big deal about the abuse of immigrants, the official would likely be tortured before their head was removed from their body.

But this is just one of dozens of stories where I was personally involved. On eight different occasions, while working as a Border Patrol Agent, I came across bodies or bones of illegal immigrants. Some had fallen from cliffs, others had died by dehydration, still others were littered with bullet holes. No matter the cause of death, one thing was sure, the "coyote" or "footguide" had left them to die. Time after time, I would run into illegal immigrants who self-surrendered to the Border Patrol after their footguide had left them to die out in the desert.

Nogales once had a Forward Operating Base (FOB) called Bear Valley Camp. Its location was so far removed from the city that Border Patrol Agents would volunteer to live out in the desert for a week at a time. Whenever I went out to the FOB, the first thing I did at the beginning of my shift was to drive up and down the main road, looking for illegal immigrants who had been abandoned by their footguides (usually women and children because they walked slower). Those that did not make it to the road, or got lost along the way, or ran out of water too soon, died.

On another occasion, we had received an emergency distress call from a woman who had been carrying a small baby. The woman stated that she was in a cave on top of a mountain and could see a major highway in the distance (probably I-19). The lady said that she was out of water and scared that her baby would quickly die if he was exposed to the sun for too long. When asked what happened to her footguide, she replied that she had been abandoned. We tried to triangulate the phone, but the results showed a massive area of possibilities. Several Agents were deployed to the area, fanning out from the best-known location on the phone. Borstar was eventually deployed, taking over the search. Borstar is the Border Patrol's elite search and rescue team. Despite helicopters and a 24-hour hunt, the woman and her baby were never found. I have little doubt that she died, her baby still cradled in her arms.

These are only a few stories in which I was personally involved. How many thousands have suffered, bled, and died crossing the border? How many more illegal immigrants have to die before this problem can be adequately addressed?

FIVE

ANTI-SMUGGLING IDENTIFICATION AND DETERRENCE

After a few years in the Border Patrol, I applied for an in-station detail called Anti-Smuggling Identification and Deterrence (ASID). Instead of arresting individuals in the field, I was responsible for interviewing individuals who had already been arrested and were detained at the station. One of our main focuses was to attempt to identify and prosecute the footguides who were leading illegal immigrants into the United States.

Every day, I came into work and interviewed person after person in a myriad of languages. I saw, heard, and listened to things that would make headline news if it ever made it to the media.

I heard their stories, struggles, problems, fears, and dreams. I interviewed immigrants from India, China, Cuba, Mexico, Paraguay, Guatemala, Honduras, El Salvador, and many other South and Central American countries. Many of these individuals came to the United States to escape nothing short of warzones. Several of them had admitted to killing people in order to protect themselves. These were ordinary people who had been forced to live in extraordinarily bad circumstances.

The footguides, especially the guides that operated in or close to the city of Nogales, Arizona, were usually under the age of eighteen. Through experience, Cartel leaders knew that juveniles were never prosecuted by the Federal government. And so, if a juvenile was caught, the only thing lost was a few hours in the detention center. Many of them would actually turn themselves in after leading their group to the designated location simply because they did not want to walk back. Apart from that, at the time, the Border Patrol was also serving Burger King burgers to detained illegal immigrants.

At first glance, it is easy to write many of these juvenile footguides off as being punk kids. But there was much more to the story. They almost all came from troubled, abusive homes. Many of them had fathers who worked in the Cartel and many of these fathers had been killed by the same Cartel as punishment for some mistake they had committed. The boys would often be absorbed into the cartel organization by the age of 11 or 12. The job was dangerous, but the reward was tremendous. A typical footguide was paid $200 dollars per person they guided into the United States. The wage depended on how long their route would take and how soon they could return to Mexico.

These "lost boys," as I called them, had already seen more misery, heartache, and pain than most people see in a lifetime. From an early age, many of them were given drugs that quickly turned them into addicts. This addiction made them much easier to manipulate. They learned from the cartel leadership and spent much of their earnings on prostitutes, illicit drugs, and alcohol. All innocence those boys once had was lost as they were exposed to Mexico's worst set of role models.

I remember one interview with a 16-year-old boy who told me that he actively volunteered to guide females across the border because it would give him a chance to rape them. He later mentioned that he had raped upwards of 12 girls, all of whom had hired him to guide them into the United States. I realized that the market of illegal immigration produced these "lost boys" by the thousands. The boys later became leaders in the cartel and perpetuated the process. By the time the "lost boys" reached adulthood, they were nothing short of monsters.

On another occasion, I interviewed another footguide, named Miguel. Miguel had just barely turned eighteen, and it seemed odd that he was still working as a footguide. Strangely, he looked more like he was heading to the club than running through the desert. Miguel relayed to me that he was partying with some friends and things got out of hand. He was using meth when the cops showed up.

I relayed to Miguel, that since he was found with meth, was a known footguide, was over the age of 18, and illegally present in the United States, he could be Federally prosecuted. Miguel's blood drained from his face. Our records had indicated that Miguel was indeed a footguide who had been arrested no less than thirty times guiding groups into the United States. Miguel began to provide any and all information he could in hopes that it might help his situation.

He disclosed load drivers and their vehicles, times and patterns of human traffickers, and smuggling routes. Some of the information was useful, most of it was not. I think Miguel could see that I was a little underwhelmed by his information.

As the interview wound down, Miguel finally put his hands up, "Alright, fine. I'll tell you where they are. If I tell you where they are, will you let me go? My mom has no one. If I'm in jail, she'll have no money."

"Who are you talking about?"

"The two girls."

"Tell me about them," I replied.

"They're in the Motel 6 located on Mariposa."

"Room number?" I asked.

"Room 147," Miguel replied, "I've got the room card in my bag."

"Why are they there?" I asked.

Miguel shifted nervously in his seat, rubbing his hands twice on his designer jeans as he continued. "I was supposed to lead them to the load vehicle."

"But, you didn't."

"No."

"Where were you supposed to lead them?"

"To a hotel called El Dorado. I had already led six others there."

"What room were those others in?"

"Room 112," Miguel replied. "I don't have a room key."

"Are they still there?"

"No, that was a week ago."

"So, you've had these girls for over a week at the Motel 6?"

"Yes."

"Why?"

"To celebrate. Please, I can't go to jail. My mom has no one else."

I relayed the information to my supervisor, who gathered up a few other Agents. We retrieved the hotel room key and got permission to enter the room. On the ride over, my mind began to spin with the possibilities of what we would find. Just in case, I made sure to have Emergency Medical Services (EMS) standing by.

With the assistance of local police officers, we approached the hotel room and knocked on the door. No answer. We knocked again. Again, there was no answer. We knocked a third time, this time announcing who we were right before we used the room key and entered.

Inside there were two girls, both wearing lingerie. One girl stepped back, recoiling as we stepped inside. The other seemed much less responsive. The girl that had stepped back from us, immediately broke down into tears. She fell to the floor, her hand covering her heart.

"We won't hurt you," I said in Spanish. These words did little to console her. We conducted a protective sweep of the room, making sure there were no threats. Once the room was secured, we checked on both girls. The one that was crying was sixteen, the other was her sister and was only fourteen.

"What's wrong with your sister?" I asked.

"She just smoked some meth," she replied.

"How much?"

She seemed distracted as she scanned the door and windows, panic suddenly in her eyes. "Is he here? Is Miguel here."

"No," I answered. "You're safe now."

"Do you know what he did to us?"

As the conversation continued, I felt sickened by every word. For the last week, these two sisters were forced to fulfill all of Miguel's sexual fantasies. They were only fed once a day, and only after Miguel had been satisfied. They were forced to do drugs, something that neither of them had ever done in the past. The younger sister was soon addicted to meth, and could barely go a day without smoking. The story seemed consistent with the surroundings. We found an 8 Ball of meth, which is the street term for 3.5 grams of illicit narcotics, meth pipes, and lighters. There were food boxes and wrappers from a few fast-food restaurants, but not much more.

"He took all of our clothes," the girl said. "And he said if we left the hotel room, we'd be arrested and deported."

"You're safe now," I reassured. "He can't hurt you anymore."

These horrific stories are all too common along the border.

On another occasion, I interviewed an older, more experienced footguide named Hector. Since he was older and could be prosecuted, he was paid much more for guiding individuals into the United States. He typically operated in the far desert, where few roads existed. He was so physically fit and apt at avoiding Border Patrol Agents, he had only been arrested one other time. Typically, footguides stop working after they turn 18 and transition into other positions within the cartel. But this particular footguide stated that he continued to be a footguide because of how much he was paid.

"You mean, you make more than $200 dollars per person," I asked in Spanish.

"Much more," Hector replied.

"Are you smuggling drugs into the United States?" Through my experience, I knew that a drug mule was typically paid $1,500 dollars for packing a bundle of marijuana, or mota as it is known, into the United States. A footguide for drug mules, however, could make much more, somewhere between $2,000 and $5,000 dollars.

"I don't fuck with that stuff," Hector replied. "If you're packing mota and run into a rip crew, it can be dangerous."

"So, why do they pay you more?"

Hector grinned, "Because of the type of people I smuggle into the United States."

"Why are you telling me this?" I asked.

"Because I messed up," Hector replied. "I can't go back to Mexico. This is the last trip for me."

"And you think I can help you stay in the United States?"

"If you can't," Hector replied, "you might as well kill me now. I'd much rather die with a bullet to the head than to have my dick cut off and shoved into my mouth while my head is being removed."

"Fair point," I conceded. "But before that's even a possibility, I need to know what you know."

"I can tell you everything you want to know," Hector replied.

"Why do they pay you more money," I asked.

"Because the people I smuggle in are each paying at least $30,000 dollars to come in. But before I tell you why, I need to know if I'm going to be allowed to stay in the United States."

"I don't make that decision, but everything you tell me, I'll pass on to the people who do," I answered.

"Not good enough."

"I don't dictate the rules; I just have to live by them." The conversation became a delicate balance of negotiation and concessions on both of our parts. Hector wanted asylum in exchange for information. It was not in my power to grant asylum, but I reassured him I'd get the information to the right people. It was another hour before he started to talk again, but when he did, I could not believe what I was hearing.

"I smuggle in people that have lots of money and do not want even the slightest chance of getting caught," Hector relayed.

"Like a Sicario?" I asked. A Sicario is Spanish for hitman. Sicarios have been known to travel into the United States to eliminate an individual who had displeased the Cartel in some fashion.

"I sometimes guide them into the United States, but I'm not paid much for them," Hector replied. "I guide them in simply because I work for the Cartel and I need to keep the Cartel happy. They pay a little more for smuggling a Sicario into the United States, but not much more."

"Who then?" I asked.

Then Hector made a gesture with his hands like an expanding mushroom cloud.

"People who plant bombs?" I asked.

Hector did not want to verbally respond, but his body language was answer enough.

"How many do you smuggle in a year?"

"Two or three every few months," Hector replied. "Not many but I make about $10,000 dollars off each one. I don't have to smuggle too many in and I still make plenty of money."

"Are you the only one that smuggles them in?"

"I know of a few others that do," Hector replied.

"And why do these people make bombs," I asked.

"Because they're terrorists."

I swallowed. For the first time, I was not sure what to ask. "Where do these people come from?"

"From camps in Mexico."

I was first confused by his answer. I was asking him what countries did these people come from, but Hector had responded as if I was asking him where the terrorists were before he had met up with them.

"Camps in Mexico?" I asked.

"They train us," Hector replied.

"What?" I answered. "What are you saying? Who trains who in Mexico?"

"Members of Al Qaeda train people in the Cartel how to blow shit up," Hector replied. "In exchange, they get priority over everyone and everything else that is smuggled into the United States."

The conversation went on for hours. I typed up all the information and relayed it to my chain of command. The report was quickly disseminated to other Agencies. Hector was escorted out of the station a few hours later. I have no idea where he was sent.

Being on ASID really enabled me to get a broader perspective of what was taking place along the border. When I was assigned "Line Watch," which is the regular duties of a Border Patrol Agent, I only interacted with those individuals I arrested. While on ASID, however, I was able to interact with everyone that was arrested or detained by the entire station. I heard all sorts of devastating stories and wretched truths. Even after months on ASID, however, I still was not prepared for my interview with Alejandro.

Alejandro was one of these footguides who was born and bred to operate for the Sinaloa Cartel. From the age of 11, he had worked as a footguide and slowly climbed his way up the food chain. Also present in the interview room was my co-worker named Juan Pimentel. Juan was an animated individual who loved to party on both sides of the fence. He had taken to living with two women, one in Mexico, who he ate breakfast with, and one in the United States, who he ate dinner with. Juan had fathered four children with each of the women, and each woman, supposedly, did not know about the other. Juan had been a Border Patrol Agent for at least twelve years at that point. Since he spoke Spanish and was the senior agent, he typically took the lead in most of the interviews. This one, however, I took the lead.

In order to establish whether this individual was credible or not, we presented to him a series of pictures of individuals. Most of them had nothing to do with the Cartel, but occasionally, there were pictures of some mid- to high-ranking individuals in the Cartel. This allowed us to quickly sift through those who claimed to know much but later proved to know next to nothing. We did not use this method often, since we did not want to propagate any counterintelligence, but on occasion, when someone claimed to be in the upper Tiers of the

Cartel, it was a useful tool. When we showed the myriad of photos to Alejandro, he was able to pick every single important individual out, something I had never seen before. Alejandro was able to provide such intimate details about each Cartel member that it left no doubt he was a higher-ranking individual.

"Then what are you doing here?" I asked. "You were caught with a regular group of illegal aliens. Why would someone of your position even come into the United States."

"I came across," Alejandro replied, "because I want to get out. I've seen enough. I've seen too much."

"What do you mean?" I asked.

"I've seen what happens to people who mess up," Alejandro replied. "I've had to deal with them myself."

"And what happens to them?" I asked.

"There's a ranch located in the North-east part of town where they take those who need to disappear."

"What is the ranch named?"

"I don't know, but it is owned by Geo," Alejandro replied. Geo was the number one individual in the Sinaloa Cartel in Nogales, Mexico, at the time.

"And what happens when someone is taken there?"

"They are first taken to a shed that is a few hundred yards away from the residence. Geo always has them tortured, if there's time. They go without food or water or a chance to take a shit. They get beaten with bats or bars. Parts of their body are removed. Their skin is burned and their body is broken. I've had to do it a few times. I've had to do it recently. I won't do it again."

"Is that why you're here," I asked.

"I've seen a dozen individuals murdered at that ranch, and I know of at least two dozen more. They don't just kill them; they mutilate them until they're hardly human."

"Then what happens to the bodies?" I asked.

"Their head is removed, sometimes their hands and dick as well. The bodies are taken to a well and dropped inside. They use some sort-of lime to cover up the stink of the bodies."

Alejandro provided more details, especially on the process of torture, but I will spare the reader from them. Alejandro mentioned the people he had seen killed and the reasons behind it. It was typically a response to someone who was either pushing illegal immigrants or illicit drugs across the border in an area where they did not have permission. But there was a myriad of other reasons as well: if they had disrespected one of the upper echelon of the Cartel, if they did not pay the "Cota" or tax that is required to run illicit narcotics or illegal immigrants across the border, if they had challenged the authority of the wrong individual, if they had slept with the wrong woman, or if they were working for the United States as an informant.

During a lull in the conversation, I pulled up Google Maps on a computer and honed in on the ranch. From Alejandro's description, it did not take long to find it. Even before I showed Alejandro, I knew it was the right location. I could see the main building as well as the far-removed torture shack and the shape of the well where the bodies were disposed of.

The interview took several hours and yielded a tremendous amount of information. After the interview was all but over, Alejandro appeared hesitant. I asked in Spanish, "Is there anything else you'd like to add?"

At this point, Alejandro became more nervous than ever. He began to nod his head as if he was trying to convince himself he was doing the right thing. It took a good ten minutes before he opened back up.

"I know about a dirty Border Patrol Agent," Alejandro said.

I swallowed and nodded. "Who?"

"Am I safe telling you?" Alejandro asked.

"Only myself and Agent Pimentel know about this interview. Afterward, we'll communicate this directly to the number one person at the station. Because of the sensitive nature of this information, this is not something we'll put in any report, or even share with our supervisor. This will go to the people at the top."

Despite this, it was still a few minutes more before Alejandro gained his courage.

"Ok," Alejandro said, "but remember, I've got a wife and two kids. You've got to help me get them out of Mexico."

"You've provided excellent information, and some of it has already panned out. I'll do all I can to help you, but you should know, I'm not the person that makes the decision if you can stay or not."

Alejandro nodded again. "Ok, a few months back in the middle of June, I was up at the big house on the hill." The big house on the hill is a location commonly known among BP Agents as ¾ Hill. On top of this hill is a dominating house with a watchtower. The watchtower is utilized by scouts, or 570's as the BP refers to them, to guide groups into the United States and avoid detection from the Border Patrol.

"Well, I was there waiting with an individual named Tyson." Tyson was a known higher-level Cartel member who had a reputation for violence. "While I was there, Tyson got a call.

"I couldn't hear the voice too well, but someone on the other end said, 'Ok, I'm here.'" Alejandro described the voice as being low and gravelly. He said that it did not sound like Mexican Spanish, but Spanish spoken by someone from the Dominican Republic.

Tyson then stepped up to the window and spotted a Border Patrol Agent vehicle on top of a ridge in the United States. "Is that you on top of the hill?"

"Yeah," responded the voice. "There's a sensor on the trail just off the front of my vehicle."

"Ok," Tyson replied. "What about in the cut below?"

"Not anymore," replied the voice. "They removed that one a few weeks ago and planted it further back up the cut."

The Border Patrol Agent then continued to drive around the area, marking various sensors as he went. After Tyson was done with the call, Alejandro asked about the phone conversation.

"That's my green friend," Tyson replied. "He's been helping for years. The Border Patrol was stopping everything we had been pushing through that cut lately, so I knew they must have changed something."

"Have I met him before?" Alejandro asked.

"No, because you're a pussy and don't have a dirt bike," Tyson said with a laugh.

"He rides bikes?" Alejandro replied.

"He's part of the RoughRiders."

When Alejandro said these words, I stopped asking questions. I almost stopped breathing. For a few precious seconds, my mind was spinning. Then in an instant, I knew exactly who the dirty Border Patrol Agent was.

"Interesting," I said.

"Can you help me?" Alejandro pleaded. "If I go back, I'm as

good as dead. Me…my family. They'll kill us all."

"Well, we'll see what we can do," I said, annoyance apparent in my voice. I ended the interview. Juan and I returned Alejandro to the large cell block and we retreated to our office.

"He's full of shit," I said to Agent Pimentel when we were alone.

"You think so," Juan replied.

"I don't know why I spent so much time talking to him," I replied. "It was a slow night anyway, and it made time pass quicker listening to Alejandro make crap up on the fly."

"Are you going to type any of this up?" Agent Juan Pimentel asked me.

"No," I replied. "It's the end of shift anyway and I'm not going to spend the time putting his garbage into a report."

Agent Juan Pimentel agreed with me. We both finished our work for the day and headed out to the parking lot. He got into his vehicle, and I got into mine and headed out of the station. I pulled off the main road and parked at a gas station as Agent Juan Pimentel's vehicle disappeared.

Once his vehicle was gone, I turned back around, heading as quickly as I could to the station. I parked and sprinted back to the detention center, taking Alejandro back out of his cell.

"What's wrong," Alejandro asked.

"You're in trouble," I replied. "There's only one Agent that matches the description you gave to me…and that was the Agent that was sitting right next to me during the interview. I think I played it off pretty good, but we have to assume that everything you just told us has been relayed to the Cartel."

"He's part of the RoughRiders," Alejandro replied.

"He's the only member I know of the RoughRiders that works at this station," I answered. "And, he speaks with a low, gravelly voice just liked you described. That's why he didn't say anything during the interview."

"Mierda," Alejandro replied.

"Now," I replied, "I can delay some of your paperwork until your situation is presented to—,"

"—I need to go back to Mexico," Alejandro said, his voice distant.

"If you do that," I replied, "they'll kill you."

"I need to go back to Mexico," Alejandro repeated.

"I'm not going to send you back to Mexico."

"My family," Alejandro replied.

"Shit," I answered. I began to consider the possibilities. If Agent Juan Pimentel was dirty, he was probably relaying everything Alejandro had said to Cartel members as we spoke. "It's too dangerous."

"They're all I have," Alejandro answered.

"I can communicate with some counterparts down in Mexico," I answered. "We can have them picked up by the Mexican police and taken to the border."

"How long have you been doing this?" Alejandro said with a poignant glare.

He was right. If we contacted the police, it would be like handing the key to the chicken coop to the fox. I considered other options, each one seemed less viable then the last. Finally, I came to the conclusion that the only way Alejandro could save his family is if he went and retrieved them.

"Ok," I said. "I might convince the Patrol Agent in Charge to do a Voluntary Return and get you back into Mexico. But as soon as you get down there, grab your family and come back to the border. Don't take a second longer than you have to. You understand?"

Alejandro nodded.

It took me about an hour to get everything approved and completed. As soon as possible, Alejandro was dropped back at the border. I watched from an unmarked vehicle as he went, making sure that he was not set upon as soon as he crossed the border. He was not attacked, at least not from what I could see.

I waited for thirty minutes, but Alejandro did not return. I looked up google maps and estimated Alejandro's drive time from his house to the Border. He could have made it back in thirty minutes, but it would have been close. Anything from bad traffic to vehicle complications could have slowed him down. So, I took a deep breath and kept on waiting.

I waited for another three hours, never taking my eyes off the Port-of-Entry for long. Alejandro did not return. I conveyed this information to the Patrol Agent in Charge (PAIC) directly. She told me that there was nothing else that could be done.

So, since my shift had long since ended, I returned to the station, got into my vehicle, and drove home. The drive home usually took 45 minutes, but this time it felt like it was over in seconds. My mind was spinning with possible explanations of Alejandro's delay, but none of them added any comfort. The most likely situation was that Alejandro was no longer alive.

At 10:30 PM that night, I received a call from the DeConcini Port-of-Entry.

"Hello," I said.

"Is this Agent Livy."

"Yes, it is."

"This is Agent McKinnen from the DeConcini Port-of-Entry. We arrested someone that ran into the port and they immediately began saying your name."

"Is he alright?" I asked. "Was his family with him?"

"He's not dead," Agent McKinnen replied, "if that's what you mean, but he's not far from it. But he brought his family."

"What happened to him?"

"Well," Agent McKinnen replied. "He's been shot in the leg, his arm is broken, and he's black and blue with bruises from the face down."

"Can you isolate him from any others?"

"Sure, but what's this all about."

"I can explain when I get down there," I answered. "Just, please, be sure and keep him separated from anyone else."

I spoke to Alejandro an hour later, but this time, I was with several more agents. Agents from Homeland Security Investigations were present as well as individuals from the Office of the Attorney General. They had told me that they had information that Agent Juan Pimentel was a dirty Border Patrol Agent, but not enough to get him prosecuted or even fired. I was told that the first time they had received information that Juan Pimentel was dirty was in 2007. At the time, Agent Juan Pimentel was allegedly smuggling illicit narcotics in his assigned Border Patrol vehicle. Despite some strong circumstantial evidence, it was not enough for prosecution.

When we spoke to Alejandro, he was a lot more subdued, as could be expected. He was not even willing to talk until I got there, and even then, it took a few minutes before he gained his courage. I hardly recognized him at that point, his face was swollen and his eyes were almost completely shut. He held his arm to his side and winced at the slightest movement.

"I got back to my house," Alejandro said, "and went inside. It did not take long for me to explain to my wife what had happened. We had planned on leaving—not like this, of course—but she already had a couple bags packed just in case. I wasn't home for five minutes before there was a knock at the door. I knew it was them just by the way they knocked. I figured if I did not answer, and they found me inside, they'd be more likely to take my wife and kids as well. So, I went to the door knowing full well what would happen.

"Before I could even say a word, they were beating me. There were six of them, one had a metal bat. I went down on the floor and the abuse continued. I could hear my wife screaming in the background, but they must have hit her because she eventually stopped yelling.

"I flipped over to my belly and tried crawling away. I did not see it, but one of them must have pulled out a pistol. The next thing I knew, my house rang with gunfire as they put a bullet through my calf.

"They continued to beat me, but I lost consciousness not long after. When I awoke, I was in the bed of a pickup truck, heading off to Geo's ranch. They must have been satisfied with the beating they gave me because they had not bothered to tie me up. I knew what would happen to me there; I knew I had to escape. When they were on a one-way road and stopped by traffic, I jumped out of the truck and ran as best as I could. While they were busy trying to turn their vehicle around, I was able to duck down an alley that poured into a crowded market. They pursued, but I soon lost them. I took a cab to a spot where I hoped my wife would be.

"We had made a plan that if something like this happened, we would meet at a specific pharmacy. I prayed the whole way there that she had remembered. She had, and she had our two kids. We headed out on foot straight for the Port-of-Entry. They spotted us and pursued. It was close, but we were able to enter the United States before they could catch us.

As the words came, so did the tears. Alejandro provided even more information than before, holding nothing back.

Agent Juan Pimentel was not prosecuted for leaking information to Cartel members. An attempt was made for prosecution, but it did not meet a high enough evidence threshold. Agent Juan Pimentel was eventually brought down through a sting operation involving over 100 pounds of cocaine, but that is another story. Alejandro and his family applied for and received asylum in the United States.

SIX

WHO ILLEGAL IMMIGRATION HURTS

The Immigrant

The principal victim of illegal immigration is the immigrant. The immigrant encounters rape, abuse, physical danger, and sometimes death as they enter the United States. But if that was not enough, when they arrive at their destination, they are abused by employers and co-workers alike. They are constantly cheated out of wages and opportunities. They are intimidated or afraid of going to the police to address these abuses because of the fear of deportation.

They find themselves drawn to other Spanish speaking immigrants in poorer parts of the cities. The subsequent generations of immigrants end up becoming predators to the new immigrants. The low-income wages, coupled with the vulnerability of the immigrants, creates a breeding pen for racial gangs. Since immigrants do not or cannot rely on local law enforcement, being part of a gang provides some measure of protection and security. These locations eventually turn into gang-ridden ghettos. Education, general wellbeing, and an individual's safety all decrease.

Many rising politicians have asserted that it is our duty as a nation to take care of the illegal immigrants in America. This has created the rise to the "Sanctuary City" or pro-immigrant laws. Politicians have passed laws allowing illegal immigrants to acquire Driver licenses, work without fear of deportation, vote, and take advantage of social services. These half-measures treat the symptoms of illegal immigration but do nothing to address the cause. On the contrary, these sort of feel-good laws actually *increase* the border violence, rape, and abuse of illegal immigrants.

This can be realized using simple principles of economics. The supply of illegal immigrants in the United States is dictated by the demand. Where supply and demand meet is the associated price (labeled P) of coming to and living in the United States. This can be illustrated in a simple supply and demand graph.

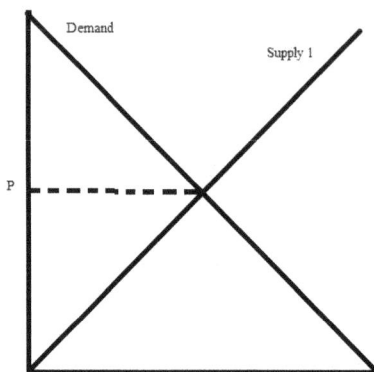

As laws are passed that make it easier for immigrants to live in the United States, the supply of illegal immigrants goes up. This is illustrated by the shift from Supply 1 to Supply 2 in the second graph.

This translates into more individuals entering into the United States and, consequently, more individuals being raped, beaten, and abused. So, although these laws have the best intentions, they actually end up hurting more immigrants than they help.

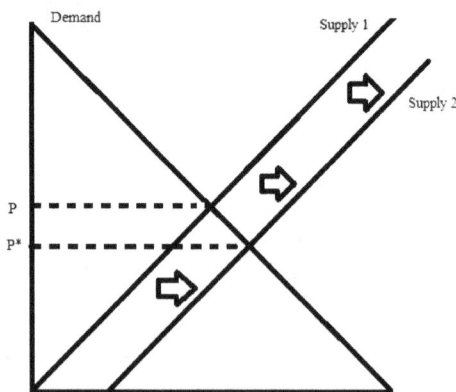

You might be thinking, if the results of providing benefits to illegal immigrants is so easily proven and detrimental to immigrants as a whole, then why do politicians regularly put this on their agenda. The answer is that these measures create an emotional appeal that increases votes. But these measures are not only detrimental, they also are short-sighted. A politician that espouses these ideals is looking to keep the Hispanic voter beholden to a particular party since they offer laws that make people feel good but never provide any long-term benefit.

The United States of America

Only about half of illegal immigrants pay taxes. Ending illegal immigration would increase the taxable base. The United States would also be more effective at stopping pedophiles, rapists, extremists, terrorists, and Latin gang members from entering. As of now, if a pedophile does not get into the country on his or her first try, they can always try again and again until they finally succeed.

Approximately 135 billion dollars of taxpayer money is spent on dealing with the associated costs of illegal immigration. Some of these costs are from the funding of immigration judges, prosecuting attorneys, and upkeep of immigration detention facilities. Ending illegal immigration would free up much of these resources so they could be put to better use.

Much of the illicit narcotics found in America derives from or is transported through Mexico. Studies have indicated that approximately 90% of all heroin and fentanyl found in the United States come across the border. Ending the flow of illegal immigration into the United States would enable law enforcement to focus much of their attention on stopping illicit narcotics trafficking.

Mexico

The Mexico Government is ineffectual and almost irrelevant compared to the immense power wielded by the Mexican Cartels. The only real check to a Cartel's power is a rival Cartel. And part of the backbone of this power base is the revenue generated by illegal immigration. Income generated by illegal immigration is certainly not how Cartels gain the majority of their wealth, but it is how they hold onto much of their power along border cities. The proceeds of illegal immigration sustain much of the Cartel's infrastructure along the border. From my experience in ASID, I learned about a hierarchy of authority that centered around an individual named Geo and trickled down to his commanders, El Cinco, El Vente, Tyson, El Trece, and their commanders, Sicarios, footguides, and drug mules, etc. This whole command structure was made possible and relevant through illegal immigration. Without illegal immigration, it would be difficult and not cost-effective to maintain such an elaborate hierarchy. Consequently, Cartel control along the border cities would decrease with the end of illegal immigration.

With an end to illegal immigration, thousands of Mexican nationals would not be raped, beaten, tortured, robbed, or murdered along the border. This benefit alone should drive even the most politically stubborn person to call for an end to illegal immigration.

SEVEN

THE SOLUTION TO ILLEGAL IMMIGRATION

After considering all possible solutions to end illegal immigration, there are only two effective (and mutually exclusive) ways to stop the rapes, the beatings, the thefts, and the murders on the border:

1. Open the borders completely, allowing anyone and everyone to enter without regard to criminal history, immigration status, or potential value.

2. Stop illegal immigration completely.

Any other purported solution will be ineffective at best, economically damning at worst. Essentially, any other solution will be more of what we have right now—a watered-down mix of laws that allows for a porous border.

If we opened the borders completely, I believe we would find ourselves in a world of economic and societal hurt that we would never recover from. Although this solution ends the border violence, I believe it would ultimately be more detrimental than beneficial to the United States. The only responsible and viable solution that will stop the rape, murder, and theft caused by illegal immigration is to eliminate illegal immigration completely.

The best way to end illegal immigration is to address the supply of immigrants coming into the country as well as the demand for those immigrants.

Addressing the Demand for Illegal Immigration

Proposed Solutions:

- Expedite the VISA and LAPR Card Process.
- Increase information sharing with regards to criminal histories between the United States and immigrant countries.
- Create a company sponsorship program.
- Dramatically increase the work VISAs and LAPR cards granted per year.
- Pass laws forcing companies to use eVerify and other programs.

Our economy is bolstered tremendously by the hard-working individuals who come from other countries through immigration. Not only does America attract some of the hardest workers, it also draws some of the most innovative. The United States has enjoyed an average 4% increase to its economy over the last several hundred years and I believe it is in large part due to immigration.

I would assert that we need *more* immigrants, not less. While I lived in Yakima, Washington, I was able to see how hardworking, community-oriented, and self-reliant these individuals can be. For the most part, these are good people who thrive when they are given a chance. We should want to fill our country with the hardest, most innovative human beings possible. Currently, we have approximately 1 million illegal immigrants that come into this country every year. I would assert that we need to generate at least 1 million work VISAs per year. On top of that, we need to approve many more thousands of Lawfully Admitted for Permanent Residency (LAPR) cards as well.

There is absolutely no reason the United States should cease being a land of opportunity for people from every part of the globe. Part of the reason so many immigrants come into the United States illegally is because the application to enter into this country takes so long and is complicated. I knew and worked with a Border Patrol Agent who had to wait seven years while his application to enter legally into the United States was processed. In the long run, he was glad he waited, but it was difficult for him as he had several friends who did not wait. After hearing about the success that they were having in the United States without legal papers, he often felt tempted to enter illegally. Currently, there are over 4 million individuals that are waiting for their application to be processed. These represent 4 million individuals who could potentially be adding to the economy of the United States, but instead are waiting on paperwork to be processed.

There is absolutely no reason an immigration application should take seven, five, or even three years—especially with the available technology from facial recognition to artificial intelligence that is able to process large swaths of data sets. Since the Federal government is so poor at expediting anything, we should give strong consideration to privatizing the process. Or at the very least, hire contractors to go through the immigration application process from top-to-bottom and eliminate all inefficiencies. Paper forms should give way to electronic ones; background investigators need to be replaced by Artificial Intelligence analysis. As an individual applies for a work or student VISA, the process is expedited each year they are approved.

We need increased information sharing with countries that have a large number of immigrants, such as Guatemala, Honduras, Mexico, and El Salvador. At this time, there is no quick or easy way for these nations to share their criminal database with the United States with regards to an individual's criminal history. As a result, we really have no idea what sort of individuals are entering our country. We need to establish these relationships so we can make quicker and more informed decisions on whether or not to allow someone else into the country.

Our goal for granting or denying student and work VISA's and Lawfully Admitted for Permanent Residency (LAPR Cards) should be at the very most a six-month process. This means that the application process needs dramatic changes.

We also need to create a program of sponsorship. With few exceptions, no work VISA should be granted unless that immigrant is being sponsored by a company in the United States. A company can request a certain number of workers for a period of time and/or season.

A program of sponsorship will have tremendous benefits for all parties involved. The employer will be able to vet their employees even before they come to the country; immigrants will have the benefit of knowing they will have a job available to them as soon as they arrive; and the US Government will benefit because they will now be able to hold companies accountable if one of their employees does not return to their country at the end of their work VISA term.

An immigrant should be able to stay in the country as long as they have a company willing to sponsor them. Over time, the immigrant's work ethic, credit, and social history will define them as a person. A hard-working individual who contributes to the community should not only be welcome in our country but encouraged to stay. *These are the type of people we want to keep in our country. These are the type of people that built our country.* After a period of good work history, the United States should help almost all individuals along a path of citizenship. The number of years it takes for someone to obtain this path of citizenship will be dependent on the individual. But the path should be available to all immigrants in good standing, to include students, workers, and family members. Additional paths to citizenship that will be merit-based will also be offered to other immigrants— these include exceptionally talented individuals in all fields and studies.

A path to citizenship would be denied to anyone who engages in or is convicted of a felony and/or misdemeanor (with a few exceptions). Similar to the immigration application process being streamlined, the process of removing someone's LAPR or VISA status should also be expedited. During my time in the Border Patrol, I discovered it was incredibly difficult to remove someone's LAPR status—even if they were engaged in felony criminal activity.

During the path to citizenship, barring unforeseen or unsurmountable hardship, all social programs will be unavailable to any individual who possesses a VISA or a LAPR card. Withholding these safety-net programs will be part of the incentive of obtaining full citizenship. It will also establish the type of individual we want to immigrant into the United States. It would not be detrimental to the immigrant because of the work sponsorship and other programs ensuring livable income.

It is important to note that this type of immigration sponsorship will be utilized through all types of occupations, not just in technical positions as is the case right now. For example, the process for Microsoft to request 100 employees to work in marketing will be the same process that Tyson's Chicken utilizes to request the use of

1,000 employees at their processing plants. There might be a disparity of pay between the types of employees, but the process will be essentially the same.

One of the biggest reasons illegal immigrants come to the United States is for work. As it is now, as companies hire illegal immigrants, they reward behavior that circumvents the law. To correct this, all companies must be mandated to utilize eVerify. The program eVerify allows an employer to verify that their employees are legally present in the United States.

But a company's responsibility does not end with eVerify. Companies that operate in industries that have historically employed an abundant number of illegal immigrants need to conduct additional checks to ensure that their employees are in the country legally. For decades, many employers have turned a blind eye in hiring individuals who work under fake papers and have illegally obtained social security numbers. New programs and software need to be implemented to assist companies in verifying if an employee is working under a false name or a stolen social security number. Companies will be required to be proactive in reporting known or suspected workers who possess stolen identification.

Cities that have been deemed as "Sanctuary Cities" will be defunded from various federal programs until they fall back into compliance with the law. Similarly, states that do not work with Immigration Customs and Enforcement should receive similar treatment.

Addressing the Supply of Illegal Immigration

- Ensure that the statistics and report data from the Border Patrol is not influenced by politics.
- Expedite the processing of illegal immigrants who are arrested upon entering the United States.
- Deny all asylum claims for the time being to decrease illegal immigration. Once asylum claims have leveled off, continue to process claims, but this time installing a cap on the number of claims that can be made every month.

- Implement new and better technology.

The Border Patrol does an excellent job at what it does. I have met hundreds of Agents who were not only dedicated, but motivated to show up, run through the desert, and track down illegal immigrants. But there is something that needs to change in the Border Patrol. The best way I can illustrate this point is with a true story.

Not long before I arrived at the Nogales Border Patrol Station, we had received a new model of Mobile Surveillance Vehicle (MSV). An MSV is a truck that has a powerful camera on top, allowing the Border Patrol operator to see for miles around. These vehicles were much better than the older, outdated system, incorporating some powerful new technology that made it much easier to get a visual of illegal immigrants walking through the desert.

Nogales Station deployed these in the north part of its Area of Responsibility. In this area, there were groups of hundreds of illegal immigrants coming into the United States. Because of the lack of detection, the Border Patrol Agents were almost always too late to interdict these large groups. With these new MSVs, however, the Border Patrol had an edge. In the first week, groups of hundreds were spotted. Border Patrol Agents deployed to the area and rushed in, making as many arrests as possible.

When a Border Patrol Agent runs into a big group and announces their presence, all chaos breaks loose. The footguides almost always begin running and others follow suit. As an Agent, you arrest as many as you can. If you are lucky, you can arrest two or three. Sometimes more if you run into some that are sick or injured. Even if you have multiple agents interdicting the same group of a hundred or so, you would be lucky to get half that number. On a rare occasion, a group that size will all simply sit down and allow themselves to be arrested, but that is the exception, not the rule. The sheer volume of people makes it near impossible to arrest even the majority of illegal immigrants.

As a result, the Nogales Border Patrol Station's effective arrest numbers dropped from close to 100%, down to 30%. Even though many more individuals were being arrested, and the number of apprehensions were going up, it made the Patrol Agent in Charge (the number one person at the station) look ineffective. So, what did the Nogales station do? Did they get more Agents to work in the area? Did they create a sub-station that could make it more effective to arrest and operate? Did they request further funding to address the increased Gottaways? They did none of those things.

They moved the MSV's. They moved them to an area were far fewer illegal immigrants could be spotted. Thus, the Nogales Border Patrol Station's effectiveness would go back up. And, consequently, hundreds more groups poured into the United States unimpeded and unaccounted for.

At first glance, this seems an egregious mistake, almost criminal, but this is a typical response to the bureaucracy and dealing with all of the "red tape." The command staff of the Nogales Border Patrol station is held accountable for their effectiveness. At no fault of their own, the effectiveness of Nogales had started to fall. With limited resources, they simply could not assign sufficient BP Agents to the area that would address the flow of illegal immigrants, and so, in order to protect their careers and livelihood, they moved the MSVs.

This sort of number manipulation is commonplace in the Border Patrol. There are two terms in the Border Patrol that are similar but have drastically different meanings: Turned-Back-South (TBS) or Gottaways. When a BP agent attempts to arrest an illegal immigrant, and they run back into Mexico, that is what is known as Turned-Back-South (TBS). When an individual evades capture but then continues heading to the interior of the United States, they are known as a Gottaway. TBS makes a station look good. It makes it appear as if the Agents effectively chased the individual back into Mexico. A Gottaway, however, decreases a station's effectiveness statistics.

Border Patrol Management prefers the term of TBS and tries to label every immigrant as such. A Border Patrol Agent, on the other hand, usually uses their best judgment as to the likelihood of what the illegal immigrant might actually do. If they escaped, but it was likely they continued on into the United States, they label them as Gottaways. Many times, however, when the Agent reported this information to management, management would change the designation to TBS, even if the illegal immigrants were several miles away from Mexico.

This is an important distinction because it signifies that the Border Patrol Effectiveness percentages are very much incorrect.

Politicians take this number as an indication that the border is much more secure than it really is. Many laws and decisions are based on the empirical data derived from these collected numbers. And, consequently, many decisions are based on misinformation.

If I had to guess, during my time in the Border Patrol, I would say that in the city, we arrested possibly 80% of the individuals that entered illegally. In the country, however, it is likely we were only arresting 20% of the illegal immigrants entering the country.

We need to ensure the Border Patrol command staff is not influenced one way or another to misrepresent their numbers. Everything must be done so that politicians and their agendas do not interfere directly with how the Border Patrol functions. Any individual that enters illegally into the United States should be deemed as a Gottaway unless they are arrested or actually seen returning to Mexico.

Better and more honest reporting practices will provide a more accurate picture of what is actually taking place along the Border. This is not only true with the two examples that I provided but in all the statistics produced by the Border Patrol.

The Border Patrol needs to continue to implement new technology to increase overall effectiveness. As of now, the problem is not so much arresting individuals, as many groups surrender to Border Patrol Agent as soon as they enter into the United States, but it is in the processing of the large number of individuals apprehended. Again, the processing of illegal immigrants is a slow and time-consuming ordeal. Through a medium of artificial intelligence and improved IAFIS, the process can be streamlined. Good consideration should be given to privatizing the process, or at the very minimum, holding a competition among companies to see who can develop the quickest processing platform. Ideally, when an illegal immigrant enters the United States, their fingerprints and eyes should be scanned so they are identified. Once they are identified, a complete immigration history should already be electronically recalled and filed. A computer should be able to complete the process, barring any unusual circumstance.

Individuals who have entered into the United States recently and requested asylum should automatically be denied for the time being. As of now, the system is so backed up, there are thousands of illegal immigrants who have not even been scheduled to see an immigration judge for months or even years. These individuals are usually flown around the country, at the taxpayer's expense, to live with family members while they await their hearing.

Even if an illegal immigrant does show up for their asylum hearing, they usually bring little evidence to substantiate their need for sanctuary. Immigration judges have so little time and information on which they can make a decision. The lack of information and a rushed decision will make it that much easier for an individual who we do not want in this country to enter.

If the United States denied all asylum claims, illegal immigration would decrease dramatically. Once illegal immigration reached manageable levels, the United States could once again allow asylum claims, but from that point on, it would have a cap. Only a certain amount of asylum claims would be allowed each month. The number of claims allowable will be dictated by the ability of the judicial system to process them.

Money should be allocated to the Border Patrol for specific tools and resources that have shown a net benefit in decreasing illegal immigration. Trump's proposal of a new border wall is well-intentioned but is overall ineffective and naïve. We already have a border wall among most of the areas that are populated. And with that wall, illegal immigrants still climb over, cut through, or dig under. Having a huge border wall that would be impossible to maintain would be more of a liability than a benefit. If someone disagrees with me, I would invite them to walk the border and see how immense the area is.

Instead, those resources would be better spent on increasing the effectiveness of Border Patrol Agents. Creating a drone flying unit at the station level, deploying a network of license plate readers, placing motion sensors on the fence, and refocusing the efforts of Immigration and Customs Enforcement (ICE) towards stopping illegal immigration are some ideas that have proven much more effective and less costly than Trump's border wall.

There needs to be an easier method for Border Patrol Agents to submit their ideas for consideration. I myself developed a portable cup camera system that I would deploy during my shift, but I had to do so out of my own pocket. There should be a centralized Research and Development Unit in the Border Patrol that develops, tests, and implements new and cutting-edge technology. By and large, the equipment and technology that were utilized when I was a Border Patrol Agent were old and antiquated. For example, many of the sensors we utilized were actually the exact same ones deployed during the Vietnam war. There is much better technology available, but for the life of me, I have no idea why it is not provided to the Border Patrol.

EIGHT

THE BENEFITS OF IMPLEMENTING THIS PLAN

The Immigrant:

Implementing these ideas and ending illegal immigration will be a tremendous benefit to the immigrant. They will no longer have to pay a Coyote to cross into the United States. They will not be subject to the violence, rape, theft, and abuses that affect almost every immigrant as they cross the Border. They will not have to run through the desert and be hunted down as if they are hardened criminals, placed under arrest, and made to appear before a judge. They will no longer have to worry about being deported for simply requesting that their employer pays them what they are owed. They will no longer have to avoid police and will be able to file police reports without fear of deportation or retaliation.

The United States

The United States will also receive tremendous benefits from ending illegal immigration. The United States will now have a much better picture of the type of people coming into the country. Since the amount of illegal immigration will drastically decrease, Border Patrol Agents will be able to focus their efforts on arresting the few that continue to attempt to enter into the United States illegally, leading to a much higher effectiveness rate. This will translate into fewer pedophiles, rapists, terrorists, and other criminals entering the United States.

Only about half illegal immigrants pay taxes. Under this new system, all individuals employed would be subject to taxes, giving an increase to the tax base.

Every day, thousands of illegal immigrants are housed, fed, and sent through judicial proceedings. Just imagine if these resources were not tied up in this constant and endless immigration judicious cycle. Federal judges and prosecuting attorneys alike could more aptly focus their efforts on charging individuals in our society that have engaged in egregious criminal acts. So many resources would be saved if the Federal Government did not have to arrest, house, feed, transport, and judge the one million illegal immigrants that are arrested on average every year.

Mexico

Mexico would benefit tremendously if illegal immigration ended. Thousands of human rights abuses being committed against Mexicans would end overnight. There would be a significant decrease in the rapes, the beatings, the murders that are predominantly being committed by and against Mexican citizens. Cartel control would weaken in Border Cities. This weakening would first come as a financial hit and then translate into a decrease in Cartel organization and effectiveness. Since some of the most violent areas in Mexico are along the Border, the overall homicide per-capita rate will substantially decrease.

NINE

SUMMARY IN THE FORM OF A PLEA

Let me end with one last story. One night, when I had about one year with the Border Patrol, I had been assigned to detention and processing. The first individual who I was assigned to process was named Maria DeLaLuz. I want you to know that she is a *real* person. A real person with hopes, dreams, and an identity. But those dreams were all but broken in the weeks before I met her. Maria DeLaLuz was only twelve, but, unfortunately for her, she had already matured into a beautiful woman.

Her father had entered the United States two years prior and was employed as a worker harvesting apples in Naches, WA. Her mother had died a few months before, and she alone became the head of the household. She had two brothers and a younger sister. Her father directed her to take the other children to a relative's house and to have her move to Naches so she could work with her father. The hope was that with two of them working, they would be able to earn enough money to pay for the rest of the family to be brought to the United States.

The father paid $1,000 dollars upfront and was going to pay $3,000 more once Maria arrived in Tucson, AZ. From there, the father had made arrangements for Maria to be driven to Washington.

As I began to ask Maria basic questions about her identity, she stared off into the distance, as if seeing something miles away. Her body was present, but her mind was somewhere else entirely. I had seen that look at least a dozen times before, and I would see it many more times in the years to come. She had been raped, of that there was no doubt. But there was much more to the story, as I soon discovered.

Through a voice that was not her own, she relayed to me that while she waited to enter into the United States, a few of the smugglers singled her out, separating her from the other immigrants. She was traveling with a family friend, but this did little to protect her. They took her to a pink house with white bars on the windows. Then she was raped repeatedly over the next several weeks by everyone from fourteen-year-old boys to full-grown police officers. They beat her, cut her, forced her to watch others being raped and tortured. She not only thought she was going to die, she prayed for it.

As those words reached my ears, my heart broke in such a way that it will never again be whole. I had spoken to women who had been raped before, but this was so much worse. It was not something I heard on the news or saw through the television. It was a little girl who was sitting only a few feet in front of me.

Maria was eventually released from Cartel control and smuggled into the United States. She had jumped the border fence and barely escaped being arrested by a Border Patrol Agent. She hid, waited till morning, and was finally contacted by phone by one of the smugglers. She was instructed to walk down a few blocks and get into a vehicle. She obeyed, but accidentally opened the wrong vehicle door at first, drawing the attention of a Border Patrol Agent. When she got into the right vehicle, the driver took off, the BP Agent not far behind.

The Border Patrol Agent initiated his lights and a pursuit ensued. The Load Driver was young, but had some experience, and led the BP Agent down a long-crooked road. The driver was able to lose the BP Agent, but then he lost control of the vehicle, sending it into a sandy berm. Maria smacked her head against the dashboard. She was not sure if she was knocked unconscious, but the next moment a Border Patrol Agent was looking at her through the passenger side window. The Load Driver had escaped, leaving her behind.

But Maria's story is not unique. It is being told a thousand times overall across the border. And as long as illegal immigration continues, so will the rape of the Mexican people, such as the young Maria DeLaLuz.

I beg you, as a man who has been on both sides of the fence, as an individual who has seen the very best people forced into hell, to demand the end to illegal immigration. It has to stop. And it has to stop now.

www.ingramcontent.com/pod-product-compliance
Lightning Source LLC
Chambersburg PA
CBHW060524280326
41933CB00014B/3091